Contents

Acknowledgments

The Central Office of Information would like to thank the Department of the Environment, the Department of Employment, the Department for Education, the Department of Transport, the Home Office, the Northern Ireland Office, The Scottish Office and the Welsh Office for their co-operation in compiling this book.

Cover Photograph Credit

Work in progress on the Tees barrage (see p. 39). COI Pictures.

Urban Regeneration

London: H M S O

Researched and written by Reference Services, Central Office of Information.

© Crown copyright 1995
Applications for reproduction should be made to HMSO Copyright Unit.
First published 1995

ISBN 0 11 701927 5

Published by HMSO and available from:

HMSO Publications Centre
(Mail, fax and telephone orders only)
PO Box 276, London SW8 5DT
Telephone orders 0171 873 9090
General enquiries 0171 873 0011
(queuing system in operation for both numbers)
Fax orders 0171 873 8200

HMSO Bookshops
49 High Holborn, London WC1V 6HB
(counter service only)
0171 873 0011   Fax 0171 831 1326
68–69 Bull Street, Birmingham B4 6AD
0121 236 9696   Fax 0121 236 9699
33 Wine Street, Bristol BS1 2BQ
0117 9264306   Fax 0117 9294515
9-21 Princess Street, Manchester M60 8AS
0161 834 7201   Fax 0161 833 0634
16 Arthur Street, Belfast BT1 4GD
01232 238451   Fax 01232 235401
71 Lothian Road, Edinburgh EH3 9AZ
0131 228 4181   Fax 0131 229 2734
The HMSO Oriel Bookshop
The Friary, Cardiff CF1 4AA
01222 395548   Fax 01222 384347
HMSO's Accredited Agents
(see Yellow Pages)

and through good booksellers

Introduction

In recent decades, many urban areas of Britain[1] have experienced considerable difficulties, leading to economic decline and social problems. The weakening or disappearance of traditional industries, the relocation of employers to greenfield sites, high unemployment, crime and vandalism, poor housing and low incomes have all taken their toll on what were once some of the most prosperous and thriving parts of the country. Often it is the inner city areas that suffer from the worst problems, but sometimes, especially in Scotland, difficulties are focused on estates on the periphery of cities.

Because of these problems, successive governments have taken steps to tackle urban decline. As a result, considerable progress has been made with tackling the problems of inner city areas. Many urban areas in different parts of Britain have benefited from this. However, much still remains to be done. This book looks at the policies that have been and are being employed to tackle urban decay and some of the successes that these policies have had.

---

[1] The term 'Britain' is used informally in this book to mean the United Kingdom of Great Britain and Northern Ireland. 'Great Britain' comprises England, Wales and Scotland.

Background

Apart from London, which has been one of the leading cities of Britain since Roman times, many of the towns that were most prominent in medieval times have since become relatively much less important. For example, York, Bristol and Norwich were probably the most important cities in medieval England, after London. Yet in 1981 Norwich was only 44th in size of population among English and Welsh towns, and York was 54th. By contrast, settlements such as Birmingham, Liverpool and Manchester, which hardly existed in the Middle Ages, did not come to prominence until the appearance of new industrialised methods of working and new forms of transport such as the canal and, later, the railway. Likewise in Scotland the capital, Edinburgh, was eclipsed in size by the growth of Glasgow.

Many of Britain's large cities grew to a substantial size during the Industrial Revolution of the late 18th and 19th centuries. The Industrial Revolution shifted the balance of employment from agriculture towards manufacturing. It also meant that many trades once pursued as widespread cottage industries became concentrated in factories. These demanded large labour forces to service them. Very large concentrations of population developed in the newly industrialised areas, with many people leaving the land. Different industrial traditions grew up in different areas, with, for example, the North West being noted for cotton, Yorkshire for the woollen industry and the West Midlands for engineering. Coupled with the rise of the large industrial cities and conurbations went the exploitation of new sources of raw material, especially coal. Areas such as south Wales and County Durham became major producers of coal.

Twentieth-century Urban Trends

The movement of population towards large cities began to reverse in Britain in the middle of the 20th century. A number of factors contributed towards this. Important among these was the decline of traditional industries in a number of areas and for a variety of reasons. Often the industries that have replaced these—for example, high-technology manufacturing—have chosen to locate in greenfield sites away from large cities. Many city centres have been redeveloped since the Second World War, in some cases as a result of war damage and elsewhere for other reasons—maybe as part of slum clearance programmes or to make room for road-building. The new housing provided has generally been at lower densities than the old stock that it replaced. However, much of the housing built since the war by local authorities, such as tower blocks, has proved unpopular with tenants, and people have sought to move out of such areas where possible. Initially this migration was towards the suburbs of large towns, and subsequently to areas beyond. In other words, suburbanisation was followed by deurbanisation. This migration from inner cities was selective; it was largely those better placed in the labour market who left. This trend was encouraged by greater affluence and one of its accompaniments, the spread of car ownership, which made it easier for people to commute long distances to work in city centres. There was also a post-war government policy of seeking to promote the growth of new towns to act as 'overspills' for the long-established industrial centres.

All of these factors contributed to the gradual decline of population in inner city areas. Table 1 shows the population of some major cities over the period 1961–91, taken from census data. There were declines in population in all these cities, quite considerable in most cases. Over the same period, many of the small towns of Britain grew in size as people moved there out of the larger urban centres.

Table 1: Population of Major Cities 1961–91

	1961	1971	1981	1991	% change 1961–91
Greater London	7,993	7,453	6,696	6,378	−20.2
Birmingham	1,183	1,098	1,007	935	−21.0
Leeds	713	739	705	674	−5.5
Glasgow	1,055	897	766	654	−38.0
Sheffield	585	573	537	500	−14.5
Liverpool	746	610	510	448	−39.9
Edinburgh	468	454	437	422	−9.8
Manchester	662	544	449	407	−38.5
Bristol	438	427	388	370	−15.5
Coventry	318	337	314	293	−7.9

Thousands

Source: Census data.

Urban Problems and Opportunities

The result of depopulation and industry moving out is that many inner city areas and, particularly in Scotland, peripheral housing estates have become run down and in need of regeneration. This need has been recognised for some time, with special government programmes for urban areas having existed for a number of years. Problems common in such areas include:

—significant areas of derelict land;

—transport links that no longer meet the needs of industry and commerce;

—high levels of unemployment, with the consequence that average incomes tend to be low;

—a lack of suitable employment skills among local people;

—poor housing;

—high rates of crime and a consequent considerable fear of crime among residents;

—a reluctance by businesses to invest in the area;

—high concentrations of disadvantaged groups, such as single-parent families and members of ethnic minority populations; and

—a generally poor environment, suffering from problems such as litter, graffiti and vandalism, coupled with a lack of open spaces for recreation.

Often, however, circumstances can produce opportunities as well as problems. For example, the upstream docks in London declined over the years as sea traffic switched to containerised ports elsewhere, leading to the progressive closure of the docks. This left many problems for the surrounding area, but it also created opportunities for new housing, retail and office developments in the area, as well as the creation of a new airport for London close to the city centre. Likewise, the presence of large ethnic minority populations in inner city areas can lead to problems such as poor race relations. However, the ethnic minority communities often have much to offer in fields such as business, as was re-emphasised by the Government at Britain's first Asian symposium held in Tower Hamlets, east London, in October 1992. Help may be available to assist such groups to participate better in the economy and community life; for example, in October 1990 Merseyside Chinese Community Development set up a resource centre with help from the Department of Employment, the Merseyside Training and Enterprise Council, and the Granby/Toxteth Task Force. As well as advice and guidance on training and employment, the centre also offers study assistance for members of the community who have difficulties with the English language.

Development of Regeneration Policies

In recent decades government policies have sought to tackle the problems of inner cities. The Local Government Grants (Social Need) Act 1969 authorised the Secretary of State for the Environment to pay grants to local authorities in England which incurred expenditure by reason of the existence of special social need in urban areas. The Urban Programme was the collective term for the projects and activities supported by the Government under the Act.

Over the years, the Urban Programme underwent a considerable amount of change as its targeting was sharpened and its priorities refined. Originally concentrating on measures to tackle social need, the Urban Programme was recast in 1978 to include support for industrial, environmental and recreational provision. It was much simplified in recent years—at one time there was a three-tier hierarchy, with seven Partnership areas and 23 Programme

Authorities which drew up an annual Inner Area Programme, and about 15 other designated districts which were invited to bid for Urban Programme support. From the 1987–88 financial year onwards, however, this was replaced by arrangements whereby 57 local authorities in England were designated and only they submitted bids. The Urban Programme was discontinued in 1992, and is now being replaced by the Single Regeneration Budget (SRB—see p. 29). Any district in England can bid for funding from this.

The Inner Urban Areas Act 1978 allowed the Government to designate areas where special social need existed in any inner urban area. The local authorities in these areas thereby obtained special powers to promote regeneration, including the ability to designate industrial or commercial improvement areas and make grants or loans within them for environmental improvements or to promote the provision of new employment opportunities.

The 'Action for Cities' initiative, launched in 1988, brought together a comprehensive package for revival in England, involving government departments in a co-ordinated strategy. This was accompanied by the announcement of new urban initiatives, for example, City Grant and Safer Cities (see pp. 60 and 44 respectively).

Present Policy
Increasing emphasis is being laid on the role of partnerships in urban regeneration, involving not just central government but also local authorities, the private sector, voluntary groups, communities and others. Initiatives such as City Challenge and City Pride (see pp. 31 and 54 respectively) foster this co-operation. The new SRB was announced in November 1993 and came into effect in April 1994, to provide a single source of funding for a range of regeneration projects.

A summary of government policy towards the quality of life in towns and cities, including urban regeneration strategies, is contained in the series of environment White Papers, *This Common Inheritance*, that have been published since 1990. The most recent of these was released in May 1994 (see Further Reading). *Assessing the Impact of Urban Policy*, a major report produced from academic research commissioned by the Government, was published in June 1994. This looked at the policies and programmes of several departments and agencies over the period 1979–80 to 1990–91. It found that urban policy has had a measurable impact on the economic conditions and attractiveness of the 57 Urban Programme areas and that the gap between these areas and other parts of England had narrowed in the 1980s.

Participants in Regeneration

A wide range of different government policies and programmes affect the inner city and can contribute to their improvement. Consequently, responsibility for these is spread across a number of different central government departments.

In order to improve co-ordination of these initiatives, a network of Government Offices for the Regions (GORs—see p. 30) was announced in November 1993. These were set up to combine the former regional offices of the Departments of the Environment, Employment, Trade and Industry, and Transport. The main programmes funded by the SRB are administered by the new offices. Many government functions are carried out by separate agencies, such as English Partnerships (see p. 15). Local government also has a major role to play, not only in the day-to-day administration of their areas, but also in promoting urban renewal and economic development.

Department of the Environment

Overall responsibility for urban regeneration policy in England rests with the Secretary of State for the Environment. The Department is also responsible for policy in related areas, such as local government and housing. The Secretary of State for the Environment is accountable to Parliament for the SRB. Among the Department's functions are:

—administering the remaining Urban Programme commitments (see p. 30) and the City Challenge initiative, and paying grants in support of this work;

—establishing and supporting Task Forces and urban development corporations (see pp. 40 and 32 respectively);

—supporting schemes to improve public sector housing, which often especially benefit inner city areas where there is a preponderance of such housing;

—overseeing the work of local government, including that in inner city areas; and

—commissioning research on urban policy (see p. 27).

The formation of two additional units within the Department of the Environment was announced in May 1993. The first of these is charged with examining the public land registers to identify unused and underused areas of public land that should be sold to the private sector so as to bring it back into use. Its activities supplement the work of English Partnerships in bringing such vacant land back into use. The second unit is to encourage private capital to invest in good projects in inner city areas.

Other Departments

Although the Department of the Environment takes the lead on urban policy, other departments also play significant parts in improving life in the inner cities. Many of the policies that assist this are not specifically targeted at urban areas, but the problems that they are designed to tackle are often most concentrated in such locations.

Department of Employment

Unemployment levels are often higher in urban areas, many of which have suffered from the closure of traditional industries or their relocation to greenfield sites. The Employment Service, an executive agency of the Department, is responsible for running a network of jobcentres, about 450 of which are in urban areas.

Responsibility for delivering employment-related training schemes, however, which used to rest with the Department through its Training Agency, has been devolved to a network of Training and Enterprise Councils (TECs), of which there are 82 in England and Wales. The establishment of these councils, completed in July 1991, was designed to build up the involvement of local businesses in the provision of training and business support appropriate to the needs of employers. The TECs are often closely involved in local partnerships aimed at urban regeneration, for example, playing an active role in all areas where City Challenge operates (see pp. 31–2).

Home Office

Crime, and the fear of crime, is a major problem in inner city areas. Overall responsibility for the criminal law enforcement system rests with the Home Office. The Home Secretary is directly responsible for policing in London, through the Commissioner of the Metropolitan Police, and has oversight of policing elsewhere in England and Wales. Police forces outside London are maintained by local police authorities, the members of which are local councillors, magistrates and independent members chosen by the police authority from a shortlist supplied by the Home Secretary from names put forward by a local selection panel.

Home Office measures specifically aimed at crime prevention in urban areas included the Safer Cities programme, although from April 1994 responsibility for this passed to the Department of the Environment. A special Home Office one-year funding scheme, the Urban Crime Fund, was in operation in 1992–93. This provided an additional £11 million to three police authorities—Merseyside, Northumbria and West Yorkshire—to help tackle crime and provide a better environment in the inner cities.

Department of Trade and Industry

The Department of Trade and Industry is responsible for regional assistance in England. Assisted Area status has been awarded to those areas which the Government believes are in need of such help. These are not solely situated in urban areas, although many of the major cities in Britain benefit from such status, including Birmingham, Cardiff, Glasgow, Liverpool, Manchester and Newcastle upon Tyne. There are two different levels of Assisted Area status—Development Areas and Intermediate Areas—and government grants and incentives are available for firms which locate in such areas and invest there. These can be quite substantial —for example, in August 1992 a Regional Selective Assistance grant of £800,000 was awarded to British Visqueen Ltd to expand a project in Teesside to manufacture refuse sacks using recycled polythene, creating 68 new jobs. More recently, in July 1994 a £4 million grant was made to Goldstar Electric UK Ltd to set up a manufacturing plant in Sunderland. Supporting a £26 million scheme, the grant will help the creation of over 400 jobs.

The distribution of Assisted Area status was reviewed in July 1993 and the Government announced a number of changes to the map. These took account of a wide range of factors, including levels of unemployment and the nature of the problems faced in each area. Parts of the South East, such as inner city areas of London, became eligible for aid, as did areas in the East Midlands and Yorkshire affected by coal mine closures.

The Invest in Britain Bureau, which is part of the Department of Trade and Industry, was set up in 1977 to help direct overseas investment in Britain. It offers would-be investors assistance and advice on all aspects of investing and locating in Britain, including:

— information on the different regions of Britain, such as transport, labour availability, sites and premises, and government grants;

— help obtaining professional services, such as banking and accountancy, dealing with local authorities, and finding potential suppliers and partners; and

— practical assistance obtaining government grants and loans.

Its remit extends to the whole of Britain. While by no means promoting exclusively urban sites, many of the sites to which it attracts investors are located in the inner cities. It has also published information specifically about investment opportunities in urban areas.

The Department of Trade and Industry used also to be the sponsoring department for the inner city Task Forces, which were first announced in February 1986 (see p. 40). Responsibility for these was transferred to the Department of the Environment in April 1992, and the programme is now funded from within the SRB.

Department of Transport

Transport can be an important issue in urban regeneration, as congestion and other transport problems can pose a major deterrent for a firm wishing to remain in, or move into, an inner city location. Improving communications is therefore a priority. Much of the direct responsibility for roads in the inner cities lies with the relevant local authority; generally the county councils are the local highway authorities, although in London and the metropolitan counties the boroughs and district councils are the highway authorities. However, the Department of Transport has direct responsibility for trunk roads, while it also has an important role in investing in public transport.

Department of Transport schemes with importance for urban regeneration include the extension of London Underground's Jubilee line through Docklands to Stratford, east London, which is now under construction and is scheduled to open in spring 1998. There are several light rail projects under consideration or in construction, of which the first, the Manchester Metrolink, opened in June 1992 and has since had the frequency of off-peak services increased to cope with demand. The Department of Transport gave very substantial grants towards the £240 million South Yorkshire Supertram project in Sheffield; over £200 million of the cost was met by the Government. This was the biggest such public transport scheme outside London approved for nearly 20 years; a line running through the Don Valley will assist the regeneration of the area. Commercial operations began in March 1994. Other more modest schemes are also supported by the Department—for example, a £100,000 package of bus priority measures in the Limehouse area in east London was announced in May 1993. It is estimated that these will improve bus journey times in the rush hour by about 20 per cent, thus encouraging members of the public to use the buses.

Not all transport schemes assisting urban regeneration are funded by the Department of Transport. For example, the Limehouse link road, which was completed in May 1993 by the London Docklands Development Corporation, has greatly improved road transport in the docklands.

In London, the Government is also introducing a network of priority 'red routes', along which traffic congestion will be combated by means of strict enforcement of parking restrictions. A pilot scheme has demonstrated both a fall in road accidents and a significant increase in bus reliability and usage. A Traffic Director for London has been appointed to oversee the red route network.

Department for Education

The Department for Education has overall responsibility for education in England. It has contributed towards urban regeneration in various ways, for example, by the City Technology College (CTC) initiative (see p. 52) and the Compact scheme (see p. 43). Funding has also been made available to raise standards specifically in inner city schools (see p. 52).

English Partnerships

English Partnerships is a major new participant in the field of regeneration. It was launched in November 1993 and came into full operation in April 1994. It has been set up to promote the development of vacant, derelict and contaminated land throughout England. English Partnerships' key objectives are to:

—stimulate local enterprise;

—create job opportunities; and

—improve the environment.

As its name suggests, its approach is to work in partnership with the public, private and voluntary sectors, and it is at the forefront of the Private Finance Initiative (PFI—see p. 59).

English Partnerships took over the work of English Estates and the Derelict Land Grant and City Grant programmes. Its budget is made up of grant-in-aid from the Department of the Environment and receipts from its own activities, and it is also eligible for assistance from the European Regional Development Fund. It is funded within the SRB.

English Partnerships' new Investment Fund, launched in November 1994, will help it achieve its aims of maximum partnership and private finance input, and ensure that its support is flexible enough to meet the needs of individual developers and projects. It will be monitored against a series of key output targets to ensure it meets its objectives. These will include the number of jobs created, the amount of private finance attracted and the area of land reclaimed.

English Partnerships has developed a new investment regime. This encompasses a broad range of mechanisms for supporting regeneration—from technical advice and traditional grants through loans and guarantees to joint ventures where English Partnerships will share with its partners both the risks and potential rewards of projects. The new investment arrangements allow English Partnerships to take full advantage of the momentum created by the PFI as it seeks to maximise the amount of private sector finance it attracts into the process of regeneration.

English Estates

Prior to its incorporation in English Partnerships, English Estates was a government agency that made industrial and commercial properties available in parts of the Assisted Areas where private sector provision was insufficient. Many of these were situated in inner city areas. For example, in April 1993 it announced the investment of £3.7 million to develop a site in Doncaster to create some 9,250 sq m (100,000 sq ft) of factory units. More than 1,000 jobs could be created over a period of three years.

Wales, Scotland and Northern Ireland

Elsewhere in Britain, responsibility for urban policy lies with the Welsh, Scottish and Northern Ireland Offices respectively. In Scotland, The Scottish Office Industry Department carries out this work. In Northern Ireland, the Department of the Environment for Northern Ireland is responsible for stimulating urban regeneration. Many of the urban regeneration programmes that are operated by these departments are broadly similar to those that apply in England, but there are differences reflecting different circumstances. Government agencies such as the Welsh Development Agency (see p. 63) or Scottish Enterprise (see p. 70) also play important roles in urban regeneration.

Local Government

Local authorities have a major part in urban regeneration. Local government has become involved in some very substantial regeneration schemes, often in partnership with the private sector. For example, in 1983 Salford City Council bought Salford Quays, a large area of derelict docks, from the Manchester Ship Canal and commissioned a redevelopment plan in conjunction with the consulting engineers Ove Arup and a local development company. Government help was also used to further much of the necessary infrastructure works. Offices, houses, hotels, bars, restaurants and a cinema have been built on the site. By 1992, nearly 4,000 jobs had been created in commercial concerns, and the total could reach 10,000 when the project is completed. Likewise, Southwark Council in south-east London has set up several interdisciplinary regeneration teams to tackle key areas in the borough in need of stimulus. Successes include the £800,000 refurbishment of subways and public space at the Elephant and Castle, using Urban

Programme funds, which has helped encourage very large amounts of private sector investment in the surrounding area. In the Bankside area next to the River Thames over £12 million of public and private sector investment has been secured.

Currently in London and the metropolitan counties, which cover the largest conurbations of England, each area has a single local authority. These are the London borough councils or the metropolitan district councils. For example, London has 32 borough councils, in addition to the City of London, covering the 'Square Mile', and Greater Manchester has ten metropolitan district councils. In other areas of England and Wales, including major cities such as Bristol, Derby and Nottingham, there is currently a two-tier structure consisting of a county council and a number of district councils, which between them carry out the various functions of local government.[2] These are very varied, covering such areas as housing, education, planning, environmental health, transport, social services and many other matters. However, those which are particularly important to urban regeneration include housing and economic development. Many of the other services which local government provides—for example, dealing with litter and refuse —are very important in inner city areas, which often suffer from such problems. Likewise, in most of Scotland there is presently a two-tier structure of regional and district councils.[3] In Northern Ireland, local authorities have fewer functions, with many matters

[2] The structure of local government in Great Britain is being reviewed. In England the Local Government Commission is producing recommendations for change— for example, its preferred option for Derbyshire is that the two-tier structure should be replaced by a unitary council for Derby and another for the surrounding area, instead of the present county council and nine district councils. In Wales a new structure of 22 unitary councils is being introduced from April 1996.

[3] As in England and Wales, local government in Scotland is being restructured. A total of 28 new unitary authorities will replace the existing district and regional councils in April 1996.

being dealt with by other bodies, such as the Northern Ireland Housing Executive, or regional boards with representation from the local councillors. However, the 26 district councils are directly responsible for functions including environmental health and the provision of recreation facilities.

Housing

A large proportion of housing[4] in inner city areas is owned by local authorities. In the 1991 census, some 28 per cent of households in inner London or the metropolitan counties rented their homes from the local authority, compared with 17 per cent in other areas of England.

Much local authority housing stock consists of high-rise flats or tower blocks which have often become unpopular with tenants, and many large estates have become threatening places as a result of crime and vandalism. Local authorities can borrow money up to a certain limit each year, which can be used, among other things, for capital works to tackle such problems. Local authorities have to submit annual housing investment programmes for government approval of their borrowing limit. Specific government money is also available through schemes such as Estate Action (now part of the SRB—see p. 45), for which local authorities can bid annually by submitting their proposals to the Government. Local authorities also have duties in relation to homelessness.

Economic Development

Local authorities have general powers to promote the economic development of their areas, which have most recently been

---

[4] For more information on housing policies and conditions in Britain, as well as the role of local authorities and other organisations in housing, see *Housing* (Aspects of Britain: HMSO, 1993).

updated by the Local Government and Housing Act 1989. Among the methods that local authorities use to bring this about include:

—making grants to local businesses, for example, to help meet the cost of renting premises;

—providing starter premises for small firms, often on 'easy in easy out' terms; and

—organising business training.

European Union

The European Union supports regeneration, maintaining a series of Structural Funds for this purpose. Among the Funds' objectives are:

—promotion of economic development in the poorest regions;

—converting regions seriously affected by industrial or rural decline; and

—combating long-term unemployment.

Programmes are drawn up to accomplish these objectives. For example, between July and October 1992, several programmes for regions in Britain affected by industrial decline were approved by the European Commission, among them Manchester, Salford and Trafford, which benefited by £63 million, and Merseyside, which benefited by £92 million.

The European Social Fund (ESF), one of the Structural Funds, provides assistance to organisations operating schemes for vocational training and guidance and job creation. The categories of people helped by the ESF include those unemployed for more than six months and young people leaving school without any training. Special support is available for groups facing particular disadvantage in the labour market, such as people with disabilities, the homeless and single parents. Many of these groups are strongly represented in Britain's inner city areas, and so the ESF, while not specifically targeted at urban regeneration, is particularly important as a source of funding for projects in urban areas. Public authorities must normally provide at least as much finance for ESF projects as does the Fund itself. Individual companies can apply for ESF money, but must obtain some other funding from a public authority. Large sums have flowed to Britain from the ESF, amounting to some £1,400 million in the period 1991–93.

The European Regional Development Fund (ERDF), another of the Structural Funds, finances infrastructure projects, support for industry and environmental improvements. Objectives for the Fund include regenerating areas affected by industrial decline, a problem common in inner city areas. The Department of the Environment has overall responsibility for the co-ordination of ERDF programmes in England, while the GORs administer the programmes locally.

The European Commission has indicated that about £10,000 million of Structural Funds support will be allocated to Britain over the period 1994–99. In particular, following a review of the Structural Funds, which took effect in January 1994, Merseyside qualifies for 'Objective 1' support—to promote economic development in the poorest regions. This justifies the highest level of Structural Funds support. As a result, Merseyside stands to receive about £630 million from the Funds over the period 1994–99.

Private and Voluntary Sectors

The Government recognises that successful urban regeneration must be a partnership effort. The involvement of the private and voluntary sectors will often be central to such partnerships.

Private industry can contribute markedly to urban regeneration by its investment decisions. A central aim of government initiatives such as urban development corporations (see p. 32) is the attraction of private sector investment into such areas, which is usually several times greater than the public sector expenditure. By locating in urban areas, businesses can provide jobs in areas where unemployment is often high and can themselves benefit by finding a large potential workforce available, the skills of which may well have been boosted by government measures such as Task Forces.

A wide range of voluntary organisations operate in inner city areas, as elsewhere. The functions undertaken by such organisations include:

—providing training places for local people, often supported by organisations such as local authorities and TECs;

—helping to provide services for many of those most in need, such as day centres for the homeless or accommodation and support to disabled people living in the community;

—setting up and maintaining nature areas and other environmental projects; and

—providing advice to local residents.

Business in the Community

Set up in 1982, Business in the Community (BITC) is a voluntary organisation that seeks to persuade business leaders that they have a role in regenerating their communities, and to involve the business world in the process of regeneration. It has helped to promote partnerships between business, government and voluntary organisations. Hundreds of British companies and their employees have become active partners in this regeneration programme, with some 500 major businesses as members of BITC.

BITC has set up a new Local Investment Fund, which was launched in December 1994. This offers loans to locally-based community organisations that are inherently viable but which lack the assets or track record to attract bank funding on acceptable terms. The Fund has an initial £3 million to lend. Of this, the Government has made £1 million available in 1994–95; the private sector has committed the other £2 million.

Civic Trust

The Civic Trust is an independent charity that seeks to look after, protect and improve people's living environments, for example, by promoting architectural excellence and acting as an umbrella organisation for nearly 1,000 local amenity societies.

In 1987 it established a Civic Trust Regeneration Unit, which specialises in area-wide renewal projects. It aims to create strategies which incorporate both practical improvements and economic development in order to boost local communities and develop fresh opportunities. So far, it has been involved in some 40 local regeneration projects, including:

—an urban design strategy for the waterfront in Greenwich, south-east London, which gained an award from the Royal Town Planning Institute in 1991;

—participating in the successful City Challenge bid with Kirklees Council in West Yorkshire; and

—providing foundation planning work on regenerating Deptford High Street for the successful City Challenge bid in Lewisham (south-east London).

The particular areas of activity it targets include:

—working with local authorities and community groups in the most needy urban areas; and

—preparing town centre management programmes to enable traditional town centres to remain a focus of urban activity and compete with out-of-town centres.

Since the late 1980s the Regeneration Unit has launched several urban regeneration schemes, supported by the Department of the Environment in conjunction with private sector sponsors— currently Grand Metropolitan plc, J. Sainsbury plc and Boots plc. These schemes include:

—Inner City Action, which helps community-based trusts and partnerships by offering practical economic development advice and some limited financial support for follow-on work;

—Winning Partnerships, a training and development programme for people involved in urban regeneration partnerships;

—Building on the Challenge, a programme which aims to increase the benefits of City Challenge to local residents and their partners through a range of support initiatives; and

—Centre Vision, a programme of town and city centre revitalisation, working with local public, private and voluntary sector partners.

In addition to schemes specifically designed to foster urban renewal, the Civic Trust also has an important role to play helping to foster the quality of the built environment in Britain. It runs a well-established architectural awards scheme, which helps to foster good design in new and refurbished buildings.

Groundwork

Working in partnership with public bodies, the private sector, voluntary organisations and individuals, a network of Groundwork Trusts aims to tackle environmental problems arising from dereliction and vandalism and to increase public awareness of the opportunities to change and improve local environments. Government funding for England in 1994–95 for the Groundwork Foundation and Trusts is £6 million. There are currently 35 Groundwork Trusts and a target has been set of establishing a net-work of 50 locally-based Trusts in England and Wales over the next few years. Although some Trusts work in inner city areas, the Trusts were initially set up to tackle problems on the urban fringe. Areas where Trusts have recently been established include Birmingham, West London (Hammersmith and Fulham), the Wirral and East Lancashire. In 1993–94 over 3,000 environmental improvement projects were carried out with the help of 33,000 volunteers and 73,000 schoolchildren.

Religious Organisations

Religious bodies form an important part of the voluntary sector working in the inner city. Because of the high proportion of people from the ethnic minorities in inner city areas, this includes not only Christian churches but also other religions, such as Hinduism, Islam and Sikhism. In 1988 the Church of England established a Church Urban Fund, which aims to raise money for the Church's work in inner city and other priority areas. By June 1993, it had raised more than £24 million and given grants to 550 inner city projects.

To assist the work of the religious organisations and provide them with a forum to discuss urban issues with the Government, an Inner Cities Religious Council has been set up. It has represen-tatives from the Christian, Hindu, Jewish, Muslim and Sikh faiths, as well as the Government. It held its first meeting in July 1992. At the same time, the Government announced that it would make almost £2.5 million available to support inner city initiatives by religious organisations.

Government Support

Government support is available to assist the work of voluntary sector organisations. Many are funded directly by local government. The Government also directly supports voluntary groups. For example, in April 1994 the Department of the Environment announced grants totalling £874,000 to 15 organisations for national projects contributing to urban improvement and regeneration. Recipients included:

—Business in the Community;

—the Civic Trust Regeneration Unit;

—the Development Trusts Association; and

—Action Employees in the Community.

Other Organisations

There are other organisations that have at least a part to play in urban regeneration and improving the quality of life in Britain's towns and cities, even if that is not one of their principal functions.

English Nature is the Government's statutory nature conservation adviser in England. As such, much of its focus is on rural areas, but it does maintain a Community Action for Wildlife grants programme aimed at encouraging local people to take action to improve their urban environment. So far English Nature has funded over 600 small-scale projects, mostly in urban areas and many to groups new to nature conservation. In 1994–95 this scheme is providing £250,000 for a range of projects, including:

—restoration of neglected ponds and creation of new ones;

—clearance of derelict sites to create wildlife areas; and

—increasing enjoyment and understanding of nature conservation in urban areas.

The Wildlife Trusts acts as an umbrella for local conservation groups. It manages the 'Environment City' programme, with the objective of pioneering practical examples of sustainable urban development by generating projects designed to test the theories. Four cities have been designated 'Environment Cities'— Leicester, Middlesbrough, Leeds and Peterborough. Since October 1992, when the quota of four Environment Cities was reached, the programme has concentrated on researching and producing practical examples of sustainable development for networking to a very large target audience.

The Coalfield Areas Fund

The Coalfield Areas Fund (CAF) was set up in October 1992 with the aim of alleviating the economic effects of the then proposed colliery closures on local communities. A total of £5 million was made available through the Fund in 1993–94 and 1994–95. This supported 36 projects put forward by 18 local authorities. In the same period, the CAF was estimated to have supported 192 new firms, helped to create or preserve 7,521 jobs, and improved 164 hectares (405 acres) of land.

Research

Research is commissioned by the Government to inform the development of policies assisting inner city regeneration and the return of derelict land to productive use. The Department of the Environment's 1994–95 urban research programme includes:

—an evaluation of the SRB;

—an evaluation of the London Docklands Development Corporation; and

—community involvement in urban regeneration.

Spending on urban research is expected to be about £1 million in 1994–95. Much of housing research also has a bearing on urban regeneration, such as an assessment of the effectiveness of renewal areas (see p. 51).

Single Regeneration Budget

The Government announced the establishment of the SRB for England in November 1993. The Secretary of State for the Environment has overall responsibility for this budget. It came into operation in April 1994, replacing separate funding for 20 different programmes from five different government departments. It aims to achieve sustainable regeneration, improved industrial competitiveness and economic development in England. It will provide better value for money through improved delivery and increased local involvement. Table 2 gives projected expenditure for the SRB.

Table 2: The Single Regeneration Budget

			£ million
	1994–95	1995–96	1996–97
Housing action trusts	88.2	90.0	90.0
Urban development corporations	291.0	253.7	244.7
English Partnerships	180.8	210.8	220.8
All other SRB programmes	887.1	777.6	768.2

Source: Department of the Environment.

The SRB amounts to £1,300 million in 1994–95. Commitments under existing programmes for future years will be honoured, but from 1995–96 onwards, as the commitments expire, the money released will be allocated through a new bidding procedure. Guidance setting out the procedures to be followed in bidding was issued in April 1994, with a deadline for first-year bids in early

September 1994. A total of 469 bids were received, and over 200 winning bids were announced in December 1994.

Government Offices for the Regions

As part of the same reforms, integrated Government Offices for the Regions (GORs) have been set up to combine the former regional offices of the Departments of the Environment, Employment, Trade and Industry, and Transport. There are also senior head-quarters representatives in each office. The main programmes funded by the SRB are administered by the GORs. The work of the eight former City Action Teams (CATs) was subsumed within the integrated regional offices in April 1994.

Prior to the establishment of the integrated regional offices, the CATs co-ordinated government efforts in inner city areas and encouraged partnerships between business, local and central government, the voluntary sector and local people. First announced in February 1985, they brought together senior officials of three government departments—Employment, Environment, and Trade and Industry—to ensure that the main programmes for which each was responsible worked together effectively. Each CAT had a small budget to assist co-ordination of government action in the inner city.

Urban Programme

The Urban Programme[5] is a special allocation to local authorities in addition to their normal resources. In England, no new schemes have been approved for Urban Programme funding since 1992–93, but existing commitments are still being met. Funding was concentrated on 57 target areas where the problems are greatest and the levels of deprivation most severe, so as to achieve a greater impact

[5] For the early development of the Urban Programme, see p. 6.

with available funds. The local authorities concerned receive 75 per cent grant from the Department of the Environment to cover spending on approved projects.

In 1994–95 the Urban Programme was estimated to have supported about 270 new firms, helped to create or preserve 5,200 jobs and supported 49,200 training places. It improved 6,400 buildings and about 55 hectares (135 acres) of unsightly or derelict land. It also supported environmental improvement schemes for 25,000 dwellings.

City Challenge

The City Challenge initiative was launched by the Secretary of State for the Environment in May 1991, with the aim of bringing together the work of existing programmes and bodies to tackle the problems of run-down urban areas. Local authorities, in partnership with the private, public and voluntary sectors and the local community, were invited to draw up imaginative, comprehensive and realistic programmes designed to regenerate key areas over a five-year period.

As a result of two separate competitions, there are now 31 City Challenge programmes in operation. Of these, 11 are in their third year of funding, while the other 20 are in their second year. Each partnership will receive £37.5 million over the five-year period, subject to satisfactory achievement of its stated targets and objectives. The injection of public money is expected to lead to substantial additional private sector investment. City Challenge programmes are monitored through annual reviews, which also approve the detailed programme of work for the following year.

In the first competition, 11 authorities were successful: Bradford; Dearne Valley (which covers parts of the Barnsley,

Doncaster and Rotherham areas); Lewisham; Liverpool; Manchester; Middlesbrough; Newcastle upon Tyne; Nottingham; Tower Hamlets (east London); Wirral; and Wolverhampton. These programmes commenced in April 1992. The second round competition winners were: Barnsley; Birmingham; Blackburn; Bolton; Brent (north-west London); Derby; Hackney (north-east London); Hartlepool; Kensington and Chelsea (west London); Kirklees; Lambeth (south-west London); Leicester; Newham (east London); North Tyneside; Sandwell (West Midlands); Sefton (Merseyside); Stockton; Sunderland; Walsall; and Wigan.

All 31 partnerships have recently produced their 1993–94 annual reports which, taken together, show that in that year:

—over 10,000 dwellings were completed or improved;

—over 13,000 jobs were created or preserved;

—nearly 300 hectares (740 acres) of land were reclaimed or improved;

—nearly 230,000 sq m (2.4 million sq ft) of business and commercial floorspace were created or improved;

—over 750 new business start-ups were assisted; and

—nearly £300 million of private sector investment was attracted.

Urban Development Corporations

A total of 13 urban development corporations (UDCs) have been set up by the Government in order to reverse large-scale urban decline; 12 are in England and one is in Wales (for this, see p. 66). They are public bodies established to secure the regeneration of their designated areas, equipped with statutory powers, generally including planning responsibilities for their area. They are allowed to buy and sell land at market value. The primary source of funding is government grant, although their presence can encourage the private sector to invest considerably more in the area than is put in by the development corporations themselves.

The UDCs in England are: Birmingham Heartlands, Black Country (West Midlands), Bristol, Central Manchester, Leeds, London Docklands, Merseyside, Plymouth, Sheffield, Teesside, Trafford Park (Greater Manchester), and Tyne and Wear. UDCs cover about 16,000 hectares (about 40,000 acres), and public expenditure on the programme will be £257 million in 1994–95. The UDCs have promoted a large amount of regeneration activity; Table 3 shows the amount of land reclaimed by the English UDCs.

Table 3: Land Reclaimed by English UDCs, March 1994

	Hectares
Birmingham Heartlands	9.3
Black Country	194.7
Bristol	44.0
Central Manchester	29.4
Leeds	58.3
London Docklands	668.0
Merseyside	379.0
Sheffield	222.8
Teesside	334.4
Trafford Park	116.1
Tyne and Wear	399.9
Total	**2,455.9**

Source: Department of the Environment.

Birmingham Heartlands

The Birmingham Heartlands Development Corporation was designated in March 1992, covering an area of about 1,000 hectares (2,500 acres). It built on the work of Birmingham Heartlands Ltd, a joint venture set up by Birmingham City Council and the private sector in November 1987 to promote urban regeneration in the area, for example, the £33 million Bordesley urban village development. This has now produced over 800 new or refurbished homes, improved the local environment, and a new village centre is currently being created. The Development Corporation has recently entered into a joint venture agreement with a large firm of developers to redevelop the 17-hectare (42-acre) Leyland Daf site that the Development Corporation acquired in 1993. This new industrial development will benefit from the improved access facilities that will be provided by the Heartlands spine road at present under construction by Birmingham City Council.

Black Country

The Black Country Development Corporation was established in May 1987. A key infrastructure investment in the area is the construction of the £93 million Black Country spine road, scheduled for completion in March 1995. Some 6 km (4 miles) in length, it will provide a high-standard dual carriageway through the heart of the area, linking to the Black Country Route, another key piece of transport infrastructure due to be completed in early 1995. Together these two roads will provide business in the UDC area with excellent links into the motorway network. By March 1994, some £580 million of private sector investment was committed to projects that had been completed or were under construction. In 1993–94 some £700,000 was spent on supporting community-related projects and £3 million on environmental projects. The Development Corporation's priority will now be to create jobs by attracting development to the 120 hectares (300 acres) of reclaimed land on sites adjacent to the Black Country spine road.

Bristol

The Bristol Development Corporation came into being in January 1989, charged with the regeneration of some 360 hectares (890 acres) of land to the east of the city centre. This area, the city's former industrial heartland, was largely developed in the 19th century, but was faced with an out-of-date transport infrastructure and a large number of vacant and under-used sites. The aim of the Development Corporation is to help Bristol compete successfully for trade and investment in the 1990s. By ensuring improved communications and a major programme of mixed development, it is working to convert its area into a thriving part of the city. By March 1994, some 70,000 sq m (750,000 sq ft) of buildings and 350 homes had been built, 2,200 permanent jobs created and £175 million of private sector investment attracted into the area.

Important sites include the area around Temple Meads railway station. Nat West Life has made its headquarters here, bringing a total of 1,000 jobs. Much progress has also been made on the regeneration of the Avon Valley; for example, a new urban village consisting of 1,000 homes and a small shopping centre is being built on the former St Anne's board mill site. The Corporation's key infrastructure project is a £47 million spine road, linking the A4 to the M32, which was opened to traffic in June 1994.

Central Manchester

The Central Manchester Development Corporation was set up in June 1988, covering a 190-hectare (470-acre) area. By March 1994,

the Corporation had attracted £277 million of private sector investment, well ahead of its government target of attracting £188 million over six years. Examples of successful regeneration projects
include the Victoria and Albert Hotel, converted from historic
warehouses into a four-star hotel; a £26 million conversion of the
former Dunlop factory, Cambridge Street, to student housing with
a £4 million grant from the Development Corporation; and a new
concert hall under construction, jointly with the City Council, to
which the Development Corporation is contributing £11.3 million.

Leeds

The Leeds Development Corporation was designated in June 1988
and is due to wind up in March 1995. It is preparing a succession
strategy for Leeds City Council to continue its work. Some £54
million of public money has been spent by the Development
Corporation on land assembly, infrastructure works and a range of
grants to improve the environment and encourage others to invest
in the area. This has brought in £317 million of private sector
investment, including £45 million from overseas. Results include
the reclamation of 58 hectares (145 acres) of land, the completion of
10.5 km (6.5 miles) of highway and footpaths and the creation of
351,000 sq m (3.8 million sq ft) of non-housing floorspace, with
planning consent granted for a further 1,700 sq m (18,400 sq ft).
Some 534 houses have been built. New business parks at Hunslet,
Old Mill and Waterside have helped in the creation of over 8,000
jobs. An important tourist attraction will be the £42 million Royal
Armouries Museum at Clarence Dock. Due to open in spring 1996,
it is expected to attract over 1 million visitors a year. The
Development Corporation has invested almost £12 million in the
project and the surrounding area.

London Docklands

The London Docklands Development Corporation (LDDC) was set up in July 1981, one of the first-generation UDCs. By the end of March 1994 it had received over £1,628 million in government grant and secured private investment of £6,000 million. It had reclaimed 660 hectares (1,650 acres) of derelict land for housing, commercial and recreational use. Over 17,400 homes had been completed. A three-year phased withdrawal of the LDDC from the area started in October 1994. The LDDC is due to wind up in March 1998.

The LDDC's infrastructure programme to upgrade transport in the London docklands is now largely complete, with the opening of the Limehouse Link in May 1993 and the Docklands Light Railway extension to Beckton in March 1994.

London's docklands can boast Britain's tallest building—No 1 Canada Square, which forms part of the Canary Wharf development. It is 243 m (797 ft) tall.

Merseyside

The Merseyside Development Corporation was one of the first two UDCs, being set up in March 1981. By March 1994, 379 hectares (936 acres) of derelict land had been cleared, 468,000 sq m (5 million sq ft) of commercial or industrial floorspace had been built, 65 km (41 miles) of roads and footpaths built and upgraded, over 2,200 houses completed, and 10,600 jobs created or preserved. Private sector investment totalled £301 million.

Among the prestigious projects completed in the Development Corporation's area is the refurbishment of the Albert Dock, Britain's largest Grade 1 listed building. This has now become a major tourist attraction, housing the Tate Gallery Liverpool and the Maritime Museum.

Plymouth

Plymouth is the newest of the development corporations, having been set up in April 1993 to regenerate former naval dockyards and surrounding land. Sites no longer required by the Ministry of Defence are being transferred to the Development Corporation, including the Royal William Victualling Yard, one of the most important surviving groups of early 19th century buildings in Britain. Its budget for its first year of operation was £7 million.

Sheffield

The Sheffield Development Corporation was set up in 1988 to regenerate the lower Don Valley area of Sheffield, an area badly hit by the loss of manufacturing jobs, particularly in the steel industry, in the 1980s. The Development Corporation's main activities have concentrated on site assembly for development, encouraging existing businesses to improve their premises with grant aid, improving the attractiveness of the Valley by environmental schemes and marketing sites and buildings. Examples of the major projects being undertaken include the regeneration of a canalside site, Victoria Quays, involving the refurbishment of listed warehouses, new offices and recreational uses, and the improvement of the canal. By March 1994, with £75 million of government funding, some 223 hectares (551 acres) of land had been reclaimed, 293,000 sq m (3.1 million sq ft) of industrial or commercial floorspace provided, £533 million of private sector investment secured and 10,000 jobs provided or secured. The Development Corporation is expected to be wound up in March 1997.

Teesside

The Teesside Development Corporation was established in May 1987 with an anticipated lifetime to 1997–98. In terms of area, it is the largest UDC, covering 4,570 hectares (11,300 acres) of mainly industrial land, both occupied and derelict. The Development Corporation's strategy has concentrated on the need to improve the area's image and increase private sector investment. Its main achievements include the transformation of the Teesdale site and South Hartlepool Docks by reclaiming land, providing services and encouraging new developments. The recently completed £50 million Tees barrage will encourage further developments along the riverside. By March 1994, 334 hectares (825 acres) of land had been reclaimed, £714 million of private sector investment attracted and over 7,000 jobs housed in new developments.

Trafford Park

The Trafford Park Development Corporation, established in February 1987, covers an area of some 1,250 hectares (3,090 acres) to the south-west of central Manchester, including a large area of former industrial estate along the Manchester Ship Canal which had become in need of regeneration. By March 1994 it had attracted private sector investment of some £719 million into the area. Some 116 hectares (287 acres) of land had been reclaimed, 722 companies had been set up or attracted to the area and 14,800 jobs created. Trafford Park has been selected as the site for one of the North West's freight terminals for the Channel Tunnel, in a £10 million development.

Tyne and Wear

The Tyne and Wear Development Corporation was established in May 1987. Its area of 2,400 hectares (5,900 acres) consists of long ribbons of run-down waterfront along the rivers Tyne and Wear.

The Development Corporation is linking physical renewal with measures to strengthen both the economy and local communities.

It has concentrated the majority of its resources on the development of five flagship schemes at Newcastle Quayside; Royal Quays, North Tyneside; Sunderland Enterprise Park and St Peter's Riverside, Sunderland; and the Viking Industrial Park in South Tyneside. By March 1994, 400 hectares (990 acres) of land had been reclaimed, £603 million of private investment secured and over 16,000 jobs housed in new developments.

Task Forces

Inner city Task Forces bring together and focus the efforts of government departments, local government, the private sector and the local community to regenerate inner cities. The initiative was launched by the Government in February 1986, initially consisting of eight Task Forces. They are not permanent; an important part of their work is to build up local organisations to which they can hand over as they withdraw. Several of the earlier Task Forces have now completed their work and been wound up, while others have been established later. Task Forces operational at November 1994 are:

—Newtown/Ladywood (Birmingham);

—Bradford;

—Derby;

—Hull;

—Granby/Toxteth (Liverpool);

—Moss Side and Hulme (Manchester);

—Plymouth;

—South Tyneside;

—Stockton and Thornaby;

—Wirral; and

—Deptford, Hackney and Tottenham in London.

Task Forces consist of a core team of about five civil servants and may be supplemented with secondees from local authorities and the private and voluntary sectors. They are based in some of the most deprived inner cities in England in tightly defined areas. Typically, these areas consist of about three local government wards, with populations of up to 60,000 people. Many residents in these areas would be those who for various reasons are unable to participate effectively in the economy. For example, this might be because:

—traditional industries have disappeared, leaving skills unsuited to the demands of today's business; or

—lack of training or language skills prevents people from taking the opportunities that do exist.

The main aims of the Task Force programme are to:

—increase employment prospects for Task Force area residents, by identifying and removing barriers to their employment, and by creating and safeguarding jobs;

—improve the employability of local people by raising skill levels and supporting training programmes aimed at specific jobs or identified gaps in the labour market;

—promote local enterprise development through support for enterprise training, financial and managerial assistance; and

—support education initiatives which improve attainment and access to employment.

This final objective was added in December 1992, following advice from independent consultants. Many education-related projects, such as adult and vocational education, school-business links and provision of training in information technology, were already being funded by Task Forces. However, the Government believes that the explicit inclusion of support for education in the programme's objectives will enable a greater focus on standards of education in the inner cities, which have already benefited from government initiatives such as CTCs (see p. 52), as well as the Government's national education and training reforms.[6]

The activities of Task Forces vary from area to area, depending upon local need, but typically include:

—encouraging enterprise by attracting businesses to the area, perhaps through the development of premises, or by the provision of financial and managerial support, as in the case of the Peckham Enterprise Centre, an independent business advice agency supported by the former North Peckham Task Force;

—identifying the work skills needed to support existing and new employment opportunities, for example, the Skill Force project run by the Wirral Task Force jointly with the local TEC, which will equip local residents with the skills needed for actual job vacancies; and

—enhancing the employability of the local population by supporting appropriate training schemes, as in the case of a scheme supported by the South Tyneside Task Force which helped 20 local residents to obtain a competence certificate in fork-lift truck driving.

[6] For more information on education reforms see *Education Reforms* (Aspects of Britain: HMSO, 1994), and for training see *Employment* (Aspects of Britain: HMSO, 1994).

Since their inception up to March 1994, Task Forces had committed about £148 million to about 5,800 projects. Projects supported by Task Forces have helped to create over 31,000 jobs, provided over 175,000 training places and helped over 44,000 businesses. They also support schemes which improve the environment or reduce crime. In the period 1986–94, the majority of approved Task Force funding—some 55 per cent—went to training projects. Of the remainder, 20 per cent went towards enterprise support projects, 15 per cent on projects for jobs, 9 per cent on environmental projects and 1 per cent on education projects addressing the education objective added in 1992.

Evaluation of Task Forces

An independent consultants' report into the effectiveness of Task Forces was published by the Government in December 1992. It studied three Task Forces which have since closed, in Hartlepool, Leeds and the Spitalfields area of London, and found that they had:

—created 4,500 jobs;

—provided over 7,000 training places; and

—advised and assisted 2,200 small companies.

The report concluded that the Task Force programme had demonstrated imagination, flair and flexibility in tackling severe problems in the worst parts of the inner city.

Compacts

A Compact is an agreement between young people, employers, schools, colleges and training providers. Young people agree to work towards locally agreed goals and in return are offered a range of employment-related incentives if successful. There are over 50 inner city Compacts, with over 100,000 young people, 10,000 employers and 700 schools involved.

Regional Enterprise Grants

The Regional Enterprise Grant programme has also been brought within the SRB. This supports investment and innovation in small firms in certain eligible areas.

Safer Cities

Higher than average crime rates, and the fear of crime, are particular problems in the inner cities. To help tackle this, the Safer Cities programme was established in March 1988 under the management of the Home Office. In the first phase, 20 projects were established, sponsoring between them over 3,600 crime prevention and community safety schemes, with expenditure to date of almost £22 million. Safer Cities successes include:

—a Birmingham estate where burglaries have dropped by 65 per cent as a result of domestic security improvements;

—a Bradford car park where offences fell by 60 per cent following the introduction of closed-circuit television; and

—an estate in Sunderland where 95 per cent of the elderly residents felt more secure as a result of improved public lighting.

The Safer Cities programme is being expanded under a second phase to enable many other areas of England and Wales to benefit. The first group of ten projects under phase 2 were started in early 1994. Two organisations were awarded three-year contracts to manage these on the Government's behalf—Crime Concern for those in Blackburn, Burnley, Greenwich, Lambeth,

Manchester, Merthyr Tydfil and Plymouth, and the National Association for the Care and Resettlement of Offenders for those in Leeds, Sheffield and Newcastle upon Tyne. The Government meets the contractors' running costs for each of the projects, in addition to making grant funding available of up to £100,000 per project each year.

Under phase 2, a further 22 projects were announced in the late summer of 1994. The following areas were invited to join the programme: Bolton, Bournemouth, Brighton, Camden, Cardiff, Easington, Great Grimsby, Hackney, Kensington and Chelsea, Lincoln, Liverpool, Newham, Norwich, Oxford, Portsmouth, Rhyl, Sandwell, Scunthorpe, Southwark, Wansbeck, Westminster and York. It is anticipated that they will begin in early 1995. The intention is for phase 2 to adopt and build on the successful concept of a partnership approach with local bodies and communities working together to prevent crime and the fear it generates. The emphasis is on multi-agency working methods, with local staff co-ordinating grant activity in liaison with a local steering committee made up of representatives from the key agencies who approve grant payments. The management of these new projects will be contracted out to organisations with relevant experience.

Expenditure for phase 2 of the Safer Cities programme became part of the SRB in April 1994.

Estate Action

Set up in 1985, the aim of the Estate Action programme was to transform run-down local authority housing estates into places where people wanted to live by providing authorities with extra resources to implement regeneration schemes. The measures promoted were intended not only to tackle the physical condition of estates but also to:

—improve housing management;

—involve tenants;

—provide variety and choice in housing; and

—create opportunities for training and enterprise.

Between 1991 and 1994–95, the programme increasingly targeted the larger and more difficult estates which needed to be tackled in a comprehensive way. Items such as the internal modernisation and repair of dwellings were not normally funded through Estate Action but were carried out by local authorities as part of their general maintenance programmes.

By the end of 1994–95, funds totalling some £1,975 million will have been made available to improve some 540,000 homes in about 170 authorities. Tenant management organisations will have been set up on some 270 estates.

Housing Action Trusts

Housing Action Trusts (HATs) are non-governmental bodies, set up by the Government under the Housing Act 1988 following approval in a tenants' ballot. They are charged with the task of regenerating severely run-down council housing estates, where the scale of problems has proved to be beyond the ability of local authorities to tackle. Each HAT is run by a board, which generally consists of elected tenants' representatives, nominated local councillors and people appointed by the Government for their experience and expertise.

By August 1994 six HATs had been established, including schemes in Hull, Waltham Forest (north-east London) and Brent (north-west London). Anticipated lifespans of the HATs vary from seven to ten years. The remit of a HAT goes well beyond the refurbishment, redevelopment and effective management of the housing stock in its area. It provides for an integrated approach to tackling physical, social and environmental problems, and each HAT is charged with making sustainable improvements to the area. The tenants, who are best placed to determine issues which will affect their lives, have a major role in the development of the HAT.

Other Programmes

The most important government programmes aimed specifically at the regeneration of England's run-down urban areas are included in the SRB. However, there are other important measures that can bring important benefits to the inner cities. Such programmes may not be specific to inner cities, but often they address problems particularly concentrated there.

Housing

Within the large cities, slum clearance was an important aspect of development between the two World Wars and in the period after the Second World War. In 1955, local authorities indicated that there were about 1 million dwellings in Britain which were in need of clearance. Between 1957 and 1962, local authorities in England and Wales demolished or 'closed' 351,000 unfit houses, while in Scotland 61,000 unfit houses were demolished or closed in the same time. In all, between the mid-1950s and mid-1970s about 3 million people in England and Wales were rehoused as a result of slum clearance programmes.

A large number of local authority estates were constructed to rehouse those displaced by clearance programmes. Many of these were along non-traditional lines, making use of tower block or deck access designs. These have often proved unsatisfactory. In some cases, construction standards were also poor, leading to problems such as damp or structural weaknesses. Such estates have therefore themselves experienced many social problems to compound other urban difficulties—for example, their layout often encourages crime, and tenants on many estates have suffered from a sense of alienation. During the 1960s and 1970s, increasing emphasis began to be put on renewing the existing fabric of Britain's cities, rather than directing population to new settlements. In housing policy, emphasis began to switch away from large-scale slum clearance towards the improvement of existing homes, whether on an individual or an area basis. Grants were made available to help the provision of basic amenities in houses that lacked them. The Housing Acts 1969 allowed local authorities to declare general improvement areas, within which they could actively encourage householders to improve their properties by means of grants, and the local authorities were able to spend certain amounts to improve the general environment. Similar provisions—although somewhat amended—remain in force today, and large-scale slum clearance has virtually ceased in favour of rehabilitation of unfit dwellings.[7] Recognition has also grown that many of the housing estates in which those who were displaced by slum clearance programmes were rehoused have serious shortcomings themselves; these are now being tackled by means of programmes such as Estate Action.

The Government's priorities for inner city housing are now to secure a wide range of good quality housing available for rent or purchase, and to improve conditions and opportunities for residents, particularly on local authority estates, through closer tenant involvement in management. A large number of programmes and government policies aim to improve quality and choice in local authority housing, including:

—Estate Action and Housing Action Trusts, both within the SRB;

—the Design Improvement Controlled Experiment;

—Renewal Areas; and

[7] For more information on housing improvement and rehabilitation see *Housing* (Aspects of Britain: HMSO, 1993).

—large-scale voluntary transfers.

While these measures are not specifically aimed at the inner city, a large proportion of the estates which have benefited are situated in such areas.

Design Improvement Controlled Experiment

This scheme dates back to 1988, when the Department of the Environment appointed as a consultant Professor Alice Coleman, an expert on the effects of housing design on social problems on estates. The aim is to test her theories that certain design improvements on run-down estates could themselves affect behaviour and reduce the disadvantages suffered by residents. Seven estates have been selected for improvement.

Large-scale Voluntary Transfers

Large-scale voluntary transfers of local authority housing stock take place where, with the agreement of tenants and government consent, local authorities transfer a substantial number of their properties to a new landlord. Most such transfers have taken place in shire districts, but increasingly urban authorities are considering whether such transfers might provide a means of generating the private finance needed to improve the condition of the housing stock. Three metropolitan authorities have consulted tenants about the possibility of transferring some 4,500 homes to new ownership. The Government is keen to see more authorities consider transfer and is co-operating with the Housing Corporation[8] and five urban authorities on a joint study on stock options. The results are scheduled to be available in early 1995.

[8] For the role of the Housing Corporation, see *Housing* (Aspects of Britain: HMSO, 1993).

Tenant Management

Tenants now have a bigger say in how their estates are run. This ranges from consulting them on the management of their estates to encouraging them to participate in taking over management themselves under the statutory Right to Manage. Some 90 tenant management organisations currently manage their own estates, with a further 100 in prospect.

Renewal Areas

Renewal Areas were introduced in 1990, replacing General Improvement Areas and Housing Action Areas as the means by which local authorities can focus activity on regenerating an area of predominately poor quality private sector housing. Their aim is to allow authorities to take a more comprehensive, strategic approach to securing area improvement through housing redevelopment alongside action on any social, economic and environmental problems that might exist. As such, Renewal Areas cover wider areas than their statutory predecessors and have a longer life, usually ten years. By the end of November 1994 over 80 areas had been declared.

Energy Efficiency

Government programmes directed at improving energy efficiency of the housing stock include the Home Energy Efficiency Scheme. The Government's policy is that local authorities should include energy efficiency as an integral part of their housing strategies.

Education

Educational standards can often be disappointing in inner city areas, with school inspectors reporting that many, although not all, inner city schools have low standards in reading.

Additional government funding to raise standards in inner city schools was announced in January 1992. Projects in 28 local education authorities were approved, costing £20 million over the three years from April 1992. These included:

—a trial Reading Recovery programme for children who are experiencing difficulty learning to read and write at the age of six, to enable them to reach an average level of reading ability by the age of seven;

—projects to build up stronger links between schools and parents; and

—projects to improve children's attendance and behaviour at school.

City Technology Colleges

There is a perceived need for young people to be better equipped educationally for adult life, and for more to stay on in full-time education after the age of 16, particularly in inner cities. One way in which this might be done was the introduction of a greater choice of types of schools. This led to the announcement of the Government's City Technology College (CTC) initiative in October 1986. Under this, a pilot network of CTCs would be established in urban areas, taking pupils from a wide catchment area. The involvement of sponsorship from business and commerce and other sources was sought.

The CTCs, of which 15 have opened, are independent of their local education authority, and have been set up as partnerships between the Government and private sponsors. They do not charge fees. They have a strong emphasis on science, technology and business, but also teach the full National Curriculum.

Training and Employment

Training programmes, such as Youth Training for young people and Training for Work, are helping many people in the inner cities. About one-third of young people participating in Youth Training are from inner cities. There are some 100 Employment Service 'outreach' staff based in or visiting inner city areas, helping unemployed people look for jobs and encouraging them to participate in employment and training programmes. In mid-1993, there were over 550 inner city Jobclubs, many catering for people with literacy and numeracy or language difficulties. In addition, Employment Service regional directors have funds for innovative projects to help unemployed people in inner cities and other deprived areas back into work or training. TECs contribute to the work of regeneration in Task Force areas, City Challenge programmes, UDC areas and other pockets of deprivation.

Tourism

The Government encourages tourism as a force for the improvement of inner city areas. Several major projects which create a cultural and artistic focus for inner city regeneration have been undertaken. Examples include:

—the Tate Gallery of the North at the Albert Dock, Liverpool;

—the Design Museum at Butler's Wharf, in London's docklands;

—the development of the Museum of Science and Technology in the Castlefields area of Manchester; and

—the International Convention Centre in Birmingham.

The English Tourist Board and regional tourist boards encourage promotional activities in inner city areas through local area initiatives which bring together the tourist boards, local authorities, the private sector and other agencies.

City Pride

London, Birmingham and Manchester have been invited to take part in the City Pride initiative, announced in November 1993. The Secretary of State for the Environment has invited these cities to come forward with a vision for their area and the milestones and outputs towards achieving that vision. To achieve this, the local authority (or, in the case of London, the local authorities and the voluntary body London First) have been invited to bring together City Pride partners (including local business, the TECs, the police, educational institutions and other agencies) to define in a prospectus their visions for their city over the next ten years, and the actions each participant will take to achieve that vision.

Capital Partnerships

In November 1992 the Government announced a one-year £600 million Capital Partnership programme, several elements of which related to urban regeneration. The programme lasted for the 1993–94 financial year. The various components of Capital Partnership provided incentives to top up the estimated £1,750 million of local authority capital receipts released by the Government from spending controls[9] between November 1992 and December 1993, to be spent on projects best placed to stimulate

[9] In general, some 50 per cent of most local government capital receipts (and 75 per cent of housing receipts) have to be retained for debt redemption. However, in November 1992 the Government announced a temporary relaxation; local authorities would be free to spend all their capital receipts from sales between then and December 1993 on new capital projects.

growth. Components of the programme important for inner city areas included:

—Environmental Partnership, which provided funds for recycling, waste management and tackling contaminated land, much of it in urban areas;

—Housing Partnership, which made use of Estate Action funding and a new Housing Partnership Fund; and

—Urban Partnership, using a new Urban Partnership Fund within the Urban Programme.

There was also a Countryside Partnership programme for rural areas.

Under the Urban Partnership Fund, some 79 new projects in 45 inner city areas benefited from £20 million of government funding, with support for individual schemes ranging from £4,500 up to £1.85 million. This level of support was supplemented by an estimated £33 million of local government capital receipts freed from spending controls, as well as over £130 million of private sector investment.

Approval was announced in March 1993 for 122 new housing projects in 103 local authority districts under the Housing Partnership Fund. The Government provided £30 million, another £29 million was provided by local authority capital receipts and £37 million was brought in from the private sector.

Enterprise Zones

Since 1981 the Government has designated 28 'enterprise zones' and four extensions. Each zone runs for a period of ten years from designation; many of the zones have therefore already reached the end of their lives. By January 1995, there were five zones operating, including two extensions. Three further zones, in response to job losses in the mining industry, are expected to be designated shortly afterwards in the East Midlands, East Durham and the Dearne Valley (South Yorkshire). The creation of new enterprise zones requires the consent of the European Commission. This is given subject to arrangements being made to ensure that state aids are not available to industries in the 'restricted sectors'; this involves the Government entering into complex legal agreements with all the landowners before a zone can be designated. Benefits currently available to businesses situated in the zones include:

—exemption from the national non-domestic rate (the local property tax payable by non-domestic property owners);

—100 per cent allowances for corporation and income tax purposes for capital expenditure on industrial and commercial buildings;

—a much simplified planning system; and

—a reduction in government requests for statistical information.

An interim assessment of the effectiveness of enterprise zones, carried out by independent consultants, was published in 1987 and their evaluation will be completed in 1995. In the light of the findings of the interim report, the Government announced that it did not propose to extend the scheme generally, although it was recognised that there might be exceptional circumstances in which the creation of new zones might be the best way of tackling a particular local problem. Thus, for example, as a response to sudden collapses in local employment opportunities, a zone was set up in Inverclyde in July 1989 and in Sunderland in April 1990. A large number of regeneration projects have benefited from enterprise zone status. For example, work started in August 1992 on a £9.3

million business centre at Greenock in the Inverclyde enterprise zone, funded entirely by the private sector. Enterprise zone status may also be combined with other means of promoting regeneration —for example, redevelopment in the Isle of Dogs, which was one of the earlier enterprise zones, was also stimulated by the activities of the LDDC.

Simplified Planning Zones

Local planning authorities have been able to declare simplified planning zones (SPZs) since 1987; the procedures were streamlined in 1992 when revised planning policy guidance was published. The effect of adopting an SPZ scheme is to grant planning permission for ten years for development that accords with the scheme. This is similar to the planning framework for enterprise zones. By November 1994 nine SPZs had been adopted.

Garden Festivals

A series of garden festivals was held in the mid- and late 1980s and early 1990s, with the aim of rejuvenating inner urban areas and reclaiming derelict land. Festivals were held in:

—Liverpool, in 1984;

—Stoke-on-Trent, in 1986;

—Glasgow, in 1988;

—Gateshead, in 1990; and

—Ebbw Vale, in 1992.

Significant amounts of work were undertaken to reclaim the festival sites and make them ready for the visitors. For example, in preparation for the Glasgow festival some 500,000 trees and shrubs were planted and a footbridge over the River Clyde was built.

The results of the first three of the festivals were evaluated in a report commissioned by the Department of the Environment and published in 1990. This concluded that the festivals had been a valuable part of the regeneration strategy for the cities affected. Uses for the sites after the festivals closed included the development of houses, business premises and leisure uses. Table 4 summarises the findings, which also included some preliminary information from the Gateshead festival. There are at present no plans for any further garden festivals.

Table 4: Garden Festivals 1984–90

	Gross acquisition and reclamation costs (£ million, 1985 prices)	Area reclaimed (hectares)	Number of visitors (millions)
Liverpool	10.3	93	3.4
Stoke-on-Trent	10.6	73	2.2
Glasgow	13.2	53	4.3
Gateshead	na	73	Over 3

na = not available   Source: Department of the Environment.

Vacant and Derelict Land

The most recent survey of vacant land, carried out on behalf of the Department of the Environment in 1990, found that some 49,000 hectares (121,000 acres) of urban land in England was vacant. Local authorities and other public bodies in England are responsible for compiling registers of any unused or under-used land they hold. Under the 'Public Request to Order Disposal' scheme, developers and others can ask the Secretary of State for the Environment to direct such bodies to dispose of particular vacant sites.

The 1993 Derelict Land Survey, published in 1995, found that there were 39,600 hectares (97,800 acres) of derelict land in England, more than half of which was in urban areas. Some 87 per cent of all derelict land was felt to be worth reclaiming. The total amount of derelict land in England decreased by about 2 per cent between 1988 and 1993.

Derelict Land Grant, which was taken over by English Partnerships in 1994, has helped to reclaim a great deal of derelict land in recent years. English Partnerships' Land Reclamation Programme, which is part of its Investment Fund, will continue to provide assistance to local authorities and others engaged in tackling derelict land within the context of strategic programmes.

Private Finance Initiative

The Private Finance Initiative (PFI) was launched in the Chancellor's 1992 Autumn Statement. The aim of the PFI is to improve the quality and quantity of the nation's capital stock by harnessing the private sector's management expertise and resources, and by encouraging closer partnerships between the public and private sectors.

The Department of the Environment's urban and housing programmes have already been bringing in large amounts of private sector investment. Examples include:

—the 12 UDCs in England, which up to March 1993 had attracted some £12,600 million of private investment in return for a public expenditure outlay of £2,800 million;

—City Grant, which since its introduction in 1988 has secured some £1,400 million of private investment in return for some £330 million of public money; and

—City Challenge, under which it is estimated that £3,000 million of private sector money will be attracted by around £1,000 million of City Challenge money.

The PFI allows the Department of the Environment to build on existing achievements through more innovation in forming joint ventures, new ways of risk sharing and of balancing risk and reward such as equity investment in joint-venture companies, giving financial guarantees, and through the use of land-value rather than cash or grants to stimulate development.

New proposals announced in October 1993 aim to encourage local authorities to enter joint ventures led by the private sector, give authorities greater incentive to dispose of their assets and unlock fresh private investment. The Department intends to implement the proposals with effect from April 1995, subject to the outcome of consultations. The rule changes should stimulate all areas of activity, including urban regeneration.

Green Belts and Land Use

Some form of protected agricultural zone around London was mooted at least as early as 1927. An Act of Parliament to promote this was passed in 1938. Since this time, the countryside outside several of Britain's major cities, including London, Birmingham, Edinburgh, Glasgow, Liverpool and Bristol, has become protected by 'Green Belts', areas where it is intended that the land should be left open and free from inappropriate development. This policy has also been extended to a number of smaller towns and cities.

The Government promotes the re-use of urban land for new development, since as well as contributing to the regeneration of urban areas, it also protects the countryside from development pressure. As well as assisting in urban regeneration, the purpose of Green Belts is to:

—restrict the sprawl of large built-up areas;

—safeguard the surrounding countryside;

—stop neighbouring towns merging; and

—preserve the special character of historic towns.

Some 1.5 million hectares (3.7 million acres) in England and 145,000 hectares (360,000 acres) in Scotland are designated as Green Belt.[10]

New Towns

An important part of urban policy in the years after the Second World War was to combat urban congestion by the deliberate creation of new towns. This process was promoted by the New Towns Act 1946, which allowed the establishment of new town development corporations to oversee the creation of new settlements. These corporations would then be wound up as their work was completed. The programme eventually ran to 21 new towns in England, two in Wales, five in Scotland and four in Northern Ireland. All the English and Welsh new town development corporations have now been disbanded, and the remaining Scottish ones are in the process of being wound up. The new towns now have a population of over 2 million people; several have become important regional centres.

[10] For more information on the Green Belts, see *Planning* (Aspects of Britain: HMSO, 1992).

The Town Development Act 1952 provided for the relief of congestion in large industrial towns in England and Wales by encouraging the transfer of industry and population to places suitable for expansion. Similar provisions were made for Scotland.

Changes in Land Use

The most recent full figures for changes in land use date from 1988. These show that in that year some 36 per cent of land used for housing in England was previously developed for urban uses. The policies are also protecting rural land; the amount of agricultural land taken for development every year is now running at about a quarter of the rate it was in the 1960s and 1970s.

Wales, Scotland and Northern Ireland

While urban regeneration policies in Wales, Scotland and Northern Ireland are similar in many respects to those that apply in England, in each there are separate arrangements designed to cater for the local circumstances that apply there. The problems to be tackled are often different from those that apply in England. For example, programmes in Wales have to cater for the Valleys in the south—areas formerly very dependent upon the mining industry, which has now virtually gone from the region. Likewise in Scotland, much of the worst deprivation is not to be found in city centres but in large post-war estates on the edge of major settlements.

Wales

Overall responsibility for the co-ordination of urban regeneration in Wales lies with the Welsh Office. Other bodies that play an important part include the Welsh Development Agency (WDA), the Cardiff Bay Development Corporation and, as in England, the local authorities and TECs. The WDA's role in urban regeneration has grown significantly over recent years; its primary aim is to use urban development to help encourage economic growth by maximising the effects of public expenditure on private investment decisions.

The Government aims to remove much of the remaining major industrial dereliction in Wales by the end of the 1990s. The

WDA may acquire and reclaim land or make grants to local authorities for that purpose. Between 1979 and March 1993, it reclaimed over 12,500 hectares (30,900 acres) of derelict land at a cost of £300 million. Clearance of a further 1,500 hectares (3,700 acres) of derelict land was scheduled in 1993–94. One example of the WDA's work is its investment of £4 million towards a £15 million scheme in the upper Garw valley to clear the site of three former collieries. As part of this, four lakes will be linked by waterways to form an amenity, while the processing of 5 million tonnes of mining spoil should recover some 500,000 tonnes of saleable coal to help offset the costs. A partnership with Associated British Ports is reclaiming 50 hectares (120 acres) in Barry Docks for a mixed use development adjacent to the town centre. The WDA budget for land reclamation in 1993–94 was some £31 million, in addition to £5 million for environmental improvement projects. Its 1993–94 budget for urban development was some £30 million, £9 million more than the previous year. This allowed over 30 projects to be supported.

Land use is also encouraged by the Land Authority for Wales, a statutory body with powers to make land available for development in circumstances where the private sector would find this difficult or impossible.

Strategic Development Scheme

A new Strategic Development Scheme was launched in Wales in April 1994, into which the previous Urban Programme was subsumed. Funding is £55.5 million in 1994–95, and economic and environmental projects will receive priority. In addition, Urban Investment Grant (see p. 67) encourages private-sector developments on derelict and run-down sites in urban areas; the 1994–95 budget is almost £8.7 million.

Programme for the Valleys

The first Programme for the Valleys was launched in 1988 and ended in March 1993. It was the most extensive programme of social, economic and urban regeneration undertaken in Wales, covering an area of some 2,200 sq km (860 sq miles) in the south Wales valleys. A new Programme began in April 1993 and will run until March 1998. The area has been affected greatly by the decline in the coal industry over a period of many years, with the number of coal miners falling from 270,000 in 1920 to 110,000 in 1945 and to 400 in late 1994 at the last remaining British Coal deep mine in the Programme area. The steel industry has also shed jobs over the years. Along with unemployment, there were also environmental and social problems—for example, housing lacking basic amenities and derelict land still scarred by the after-effects of mining. Special measures were therefore needed to address the problems.

The new Programme for the Valleys involves increased levels of factory building, land clearance and domestic and European Union funding, as well as action to:

—stimulate private enterprise;

—generate a diverse and sustainable economy;

—create more better-quality jobs;

—improve training, educational and health care services;

—support private housing improvements; and

—strengthen tourism, the arts and voluntary organisations.

Some £17 million of Urban Programme support benefited the Valleys in 1993–94, or about 60 per cent of total Urban Programme spending in Wales. Other parts of the Programme include special loans schemes for Valleys businesses provided by the WDA in association with major clearing banks, a major expansion of the

WDA's factory building programme, and a continuation of the WDA's derelict land reclamation programme.

The first Programme's successes include:

—the improvement of over 7,000 homes;

—the clearance of over 800 hectares (2,000 acres) of derelict land by the WDA;

—the securing of nearly £700 million of additional private sector investment, creating or safeguarding 24,000 jobs;

—the creation of 240,000 sq m (2.6 million sq ft) of new industrial floorspace; and

—the 1992 National Garden Festival at Ebbw Vale.

The new Programme will involve public spending of well over £1,000 million. It is intended that the emphasis of the Programme will be shifted from centralised initiatives to local partnerships and strategies and also on to developing links with other areas in the European Union. In order to encourage the development of employment opportunities, the Government is encouraging local authorities in the Valleys to make full use of SPZ procedures (see p. 57).

Cardiff Bay Development Corporation

The Cardiff Bay Development Corporation was set up in 1987 to bring forward redevelopment in an area of south Cardiff, once its commercial centre. By August 1994 the Corporation had received £220 million in government grant. Government provision for the Corporation in 1994–95 will be £48 million.

The Corporation's regeneration strategy includes the construction of a barrage across Cardiff harbour mouth, which will create a large freshwater lake and 12 km (7 miles) of waterside frontage. Work on this project started in June 1994 and is due to be completed in 1998. It is anticipated that over £1,200 million of private investment will be attracted. The latest economic impact study anticipates that about 23,000 new jobs will be created and some 440,000 sq m (4.7 million sq ft) of business space created. Without the barrage, these figures would be roughly halved.

Other Measures

The Government has taken a number of other measures to promote urban regeneration in Wales, often in partnership with other bodies. For example, in March 1993 the Tredegar Action Group was launched to revitalise the Tredegar area. As well as the Government, this involved the WDA, the local community and the private sector. As part of this, an extra government aid allocation of £300,000 in 1993–94 to Tredegar was announced, with the proviso that the projects covered by this allocation were linked to a viable strategy. Likewise, in August 1992 a £3 million joint venture between the WDA and Arfon Borough Council was announced, aiming to regenerate the Victoria Dock, Caernarfon. The waterfront scheme, which will include commercial development, tourist facilities and car parking on a 4-hectare (10-acre) site, is intended to bring in some £8 million of private sector investment. It forms part of a joint regeneration strategy drawn up between the WDA, the borough council and Gwynedd County Council.

Private sector investment can be encouraged by means of Urban Investment Grant, a scheme which is designed to promote development on derelict urban sites where there is a gap between the development cost of a project and its commercial value on completion. For example, between January 1992 and June 1993, grant was approved for:

—the construction of 6,100 sq m (65,000 sq ft) of office accommodation at Merthyr Tydfil, costing some £4.7 million and supported by £1.3 million of grant;

—a £5 million office development in Swansea, assisted by a
£500,000 grant;

—the purchase of factory and office units at Caerffili, aided by a
£136,000 grant; and

—a retail and office development at Colwyn Bay costing some
£1 million and supported by a £200,000 grant.

The Government announced Urban Investment Grant for 11
development projects in the first six months of 1994. Public
support of nearly £8 million will secure more than £45 million of
private investment and create about 950 permanent jobs.

Scotland

The Scottish Office has overall responsibility for urban regeneration policy in Scotland.

New Life for Urban Scotland

In 1988 the Government set out in the White Paper *New Life for
Urban Scotland* its strategy for improving the quality of life for
people living on peripheral estates in Scotland. Building on the
experience gained from inner city regeneration schemes such as the
Glasgow Eastern Area Renewal project, an important aim of the
strategy was to encourage residents to take more responsibility for
the improvement of their own communities.

A focus of this effort was the establishment of four Urban
Partnerships in housing estates on the outskirts of Dundee,
Edinburgh, Glasgow and Paisley. These are led by The Scottish

Office, working in partnership with other bodies and local groups, including local enterprise companies, Scottish Homes (see p. 71), local authorities, the private sector and local communities. Their objectives include plans to:

—improve employment prospects by providing increased avenues for training and further education;

—tackle social and environmental problems on the estates; and

—improve the type and tenure mix of housing available to local people.

Almost 30 per cent of the housing stock in the Partnership areas has now been renovated, with over 6,500 homes refurbished and 1,300 new homes built. Local authority ownership has declined from 97 per cent to 73 per cent, with owner-occupation increasing from 2.5 per cent to 10 per cent and community ownership from less than 1 per cent to 12 per cent.

Smaller Urban Renewal Initiatives

The four Urban Partnerships form only part of the area-based urban regeneration work in Scotland. Smaller Urban Renewal Initiatives (SURIs) aim to promote, through housing-led initiatives, sustainable regeneration in smaller estates outside the cities and main urban areas. Led by Scottish Homes, SURIs follow much of the approach adopted by the Urban Partnerships and involve the same key partners. They aim to ensure that an integrated approach is developed so that resources are used to best effect to assist the communities in becoming self-sustaining. The first SURIs were approved in 1990. A total of 11 have now been created, varying in size from around 500 dwellings to over 3,500. The regeneration programmes for each area are expected to take three to five years. Scottish Homes is investing £24 million in the SURIs in 1994–95.

Review of Urban Regeneration Policy

A review of urban regeneration policy in Scotland was launched in October 1993. In January 1995 the Government announced the findings. It will encourage the formation of city or district-wide partnerships in areas with significant concentrations of deprivation. These will involve as partners the local authorities, Scottish Homes and the local enterprise companies (LECs—see below) and others. The partnerships will aim to produce regeneration strategies at city or district level, and to develop more localised proposals for priority areas. About two-thirds of Urban Programme resources will in future be allocated to priority partnership areas, to be designated by The Scottish Office following discussions with city and district partnerships. The remainder will be available to support regeneration activity in other eligible disadvantaged areas. In both cases, allocations will take account of need and the quality of the proposals submitted.

Scottish Enterprise

Scottish Enterprise plays an important part in urban regeneration. The bulk of activity and expenditure is contracted out to a network of 22 LECs. These range in size from the Glasgow Development Agency, with 156 staff and an annual budget of £54 million to Scottish Borders Enterprise, with about 30 staff and a budget of £8.5 million. The LECs are led by chairmen and boards drawn from their localities, at least two-thirds of whom must be from the private sector. They have substantial delegated authority and the flexibility to shape projects and programmes so as best to suit the needs of the area. Scottish Enterprise and the LECs undertake a very wide range of projects and programmes. These include:

—advice and information for new and small firms;

—assistance to unemployed people wishing to become self-employed;

—help for companies in meeting property, investment, marketing and training needs;

—Youth Training, leading to recognised vocational qualifications, for all young people leaving school who do not have a job and who are not going into further or higher education;

—Training for Work, designed to help adults who have been unemployed for six months or more to acquire skills, brush up existing work expertise and to find jobs;

—the reclamation of derelict and polluted land; and

—local environment projects, for example, landscaping projects.

Scottish Enterprise operates Local Enterprise Grants for Urban Projects, a scheme which aims to encourage private sector investment for projects in deprived areas. The areas of need in which the scheme operates include the four Partnership areas, as well as other areas showing similar characteristics of deprivation. The LECs can also support projects in their areas.

Scottish Homes

Given the nature of Scotland's deprived urban areas, revitalising housing is especially important. Since its creation in 1989, Scottish Homes, which is broadly equivalent to the Housing Corporation in England, has played a valuable role in urban regeneration in Scotland. Central to its remit are the aims to improve housing supply and quality, widen choices for owners and tenants, and stimulate private investment. Scottish Homes encourages a co-ordinated approach to urban regeneration, recognising the need to involve councils, the private sector and local communities. Apart from its role in the Partnerships and the SURIs, Scottish Homes' spread of activities is diverse, from work in older urban neighbourhoods mainly in Edinburgh, Glasgow and Dundee to improvement of newer peripheral estates such as Forgewood in Motherwell. The main objective remains the achievement of self-sustaining regeneration in a wide variety of urban communities.

Crime and Safety

The Scottish Safer Cities Programme was established in 1989 to illustrate the value of tackling crime, the fear of crime and other safety issues in inner cities and urban areas, through community-based inter-agency projects. Five projects were established—in Edinburgh city centre; Castlemilk and Greater Easterhouse, Glasgow; north-east Dundee; and north-east Aberdeen. Four of these are still operational. The projects are centrally funded, with a total allocation of £855,000 for 1994–95. Initiatives undertaken by the projects include:

—the installation of smoke alarms in 2,000 households in the Easterhouse area of Glasgow;

—a drama workshop touring secondary schools in Lothian warning children of the dangers of alcohol abuse;

—the production of a *Safe Taysider* comic, which was distributed free to 33,000 schoolchildren in Dundee; and

—a 'Pass to Safe Play' scheme within Castlemilk, in conjunction with Glasgow City Council, which provided affordable leisure opportunities to 3,500 schoolchildren, helping to direct them away from anti-social, criminal or dangerous behaviour.

Other Measures

Other peripheral estates and inner city areas continue to receive substantial support through such sources as the Urban Programme and Scottish Enterprise and its network of local enterprise companies. The Government is committed to seeking ways to improve the Partnerships and to strengthening the Urban Programme in Scotland by emphasising those projects which form part of a concerted effort to assist a deprived area.

The Urban Programme in Scotland has grown from £44 million in 1988–89 to over £85 million in 1994–95. New projects announced for 1993–94 included, for example:

—an out-of-school project in Stirling to provide child care after school to assist parents who are actively seeking employment;

—a voluntary project in Kirkcaldy to prevent family breakdown while increasing people's independence within their families;

—an enterprise workshop at Broxburn, Lothian, which will provide a complex of managed workspaces and is likely to create about 30 jobs;

—an information technology bus which will provide a mobile training facility in north Glasgow to assist small businesses; and

—a resource centre in Greenock, which will provide local residents with access to a wide range of services such as debt counselling, information on adult education and help with job seeking.

The Compact scheme (see p. 43) is now well developed in Scotland, with 12 Compacts in operation. Some 7,400 young people are involved with the operational Compacts, as well as many employers.

Northern Ireland

Considerable public expenditure is being devoted to the regeneration of Belfast and Londonderry. In 1993–94 regeneration programmes had a combined allocation of over £34 million. Private sector initiatives are encouraged by the Urban Development Grant scheme, which by the end of June 1993 had contributed £71 million to projects that brought in £273 million of private sector investment.

Belfast

A comprehensive development programme aims to revitalise the commercial areas of Belfast. Nine Action Teams have been established to tackle the problems of particularly deprived areas of the city.

The 'Making Belfast Work' initiative, launched in 1988, is designed to reinforce the efforts to alleviate the economic, educational, social and environmental problems in the most disadvantaged areas of Belfast. In addition to extensive funding already allocated to mainstream departmental programmes, Making Belfast Work has provided a further £144 million for the period 1988–89 to 1994–95. The budget for the programme in 1994–95 is £24.6 million.

Laganside Corporation

The Laganside Corporation was established in 1989 to regenerate Belfast's riverside area, which is at the heart of Belfast. Its government grant in 1993–94 was £5.3 million. Work is either completed or under way on five development sites along the banks of the river, including the Laganbank scheme, comprising offices, shops, hotel, car parking and a hall for conferences and concerts.

Londonderry

The Londonderry Initiative was launched in 1988. It consists of three main elements:

—a town centre development programme, aimed at encouraging private sector investment in new shops, offices and other facilities;

—a community action programme, to create more job opportunities and increase the employability of people in the most disadvantaged areas of the city; and

—a promotional strategy for the city, which culminated in 1992 in a major festival of local, national and international events.

Other developments within Londonderry include restoration work within the walled city, the relocation of harbour facilities along the River Foyle, and the construction of government offices at Dorman's Wharf and in the Foyle Street area of Londonderry.

In May 1993 work commenced on a £65 million retail development in the Foyle Street area of Londonderry. This is the most extensive single development ever carried out in the centre of the city and will provide 18,700 sq m (200,000 sq ft) of retail sales space and multi-storey parking for 1,300 cars.

Safer Towns

Three Safer Towns initiatives have been launched in Northern Ireland, operating in south Belfast, Lisburn and Newtownabbey. They are run under the aegis of the Extern Organisation, an established crime prevention group.

Community Regeneration and Improvement Special Programme

The Community Regeneration and Improvement Special Programme aims to regenerate disadvantaged smaller towns. It is

jointly funded by the Department of the Environment for
Northern Ireland and the International Fund for Ireland. A total of
33 small towns have been helped since the programme was started
in 1990.

Addresses

Government Departments and Agencies

Department of the Environment, 2 Marsham Street, London SW1P 3EB.

Department of Trade and Industry, Ashdown House, 123 Victoria Street, London SW1E 6RB.

Northern Ireland Office, Parliament Buildings, Stormont, Belfast BT4 3ST.

Scottish Enterprise, 120 Bothwell Street, Glasgow G2 7JP.

The Scottish Office Industry Department, New St Andrew's House, Edinburgh EH1 3TG.

Welsh Development Agency, Pearl House, Greyfriars Road, Cardiff CF1 3XX.

Welsh Office, Cathays Park, Cardiff CF1 3NQ.

Urban Development Corporations

Birmingham Heartlands Development Corporation, 43 Waterlinks House, Richard Street, Birmingham B7 4AA.

Black Country Development Corporation, Black Country House, Rounds Green, Oldbury, West Midlands B69 2DG.

Bristol Development Corporation, Techno House, Redcliffe Way, Bristol BS1 6NX.

Cardiff Bay Development Corporation, Baltic House, Mount Stuart Square, Cardiff CF1 6DH.

Central Manchester Development Corporation, Churchgate House, 56 Oxford Street, Manchester M1 6EU.

Leeds Development Corporation, South Point, South Accommodation Road, Leeds LS10 1PP.

London Docklands Development Corporation, Thames Quay, 191 Marsh Wall, London E14 9TJ.

Merseyside Development Corporation, Royal Liver Building, Pier Head, Liverpool L3 1JH.

Plymouth Development Corporation, 1 Royal William Yard, Plymouth PL1 3RP.

Sheffield Development Corporation, Don Valley House, Savile Street East, Sheffield S4 7UQ.

Teesside Development Corporation, Tees House, Riverside Park, Middlesbrough, Cleveland TS2 1RE.

Trafford Park Development Corporation, Trafford Wharf Road, Wharfside, Trafford Park, Manchester M17 1EX.

Tyne and Wear Development Corporation, Scotswood House, Newcastle Business Park, Newcastle upon Tyne NE4 7YL.

Other Organisations

Business in the Community, 227a City Road, London EC1V 1LX.

Civic Trust, 17 Carlton House Terrace, London SW1Y 5AW.

Groundwork Foundation, 85–87 Cornwall Street, Birmingham B3 3BY.

Further Reading

			£
Assessing the Impact of Urban Policy. ISBN 0 11 752983 6.	HMSO	1994	40.00
City Action—People in Partnership.	Department of Employment	1993	Free
Crime Prevention on Council Estates. ISBN 0 11 752766 1.	HMSO	1993	12.00
National Sample Survey of Vacant Urban Land in England 1990. ISBN 0 11 752692 4.	HMSO	1992	22.00
Task Forces in Action.	Department of the Environment	1993	Free
This Common Inheritance: the Third Year Report. Cm 2549. ISBN 0 10 125492 X.	HMSO	1994	21.00

Abbreviations

BITC	Business in the Community
CAF	Coalfield Areas Fund
CTC	City Technology College
ERDF	European Regional Development Fund
ESF	European Social Fund
GOR	Government Office for the Regions
HAT	Housing Action Trust
LDDC	London Docklands Development Corporation
LEC	Local enterprise company
PFI	Private Finance Initiative
SPZ	Simplified planning zone
SRB	Single Regeneration Budget
SURI	Smaller Urban Renewal Initiative
TEC	Training and Enterprise Council
UDC	Urban development corporation
WDA	Welsh Development Agency

Index

Transport, Department of 9, 13–4, 30

Tyne and Wear 39–40

Urban Crime Fund 11–12
Urban decline 1
Urban development corporations (UDCs) 22, 32–40, 53, 59
land reclaimed in England (table) 33
Urban Partnerships 55, 68, 69
Fund 55
Urban Programme 5, 6, 7, 8, 9, 17–8, 30–1, 55, 64, 65, 70, 73
Urban regeneration 7, 11, 14, 15, 17, 18, 21–2, 28, 34, 63, 67, 71–2
policy 7–8

Voluntary groups 7
Voluntary sector 21–6, 30, 31, 41
government support 26

Voluntary transfers 50

Wales 2, 11, 17, 18, 24, 32, 44, 48, 62, 63–8
Programme for the Valleys 65
Strategic Development Scheme 64
Tredegar Action Group 67
Urban Investment Grant 64, 67–8
Welsh Development Agency 63–4, 65–6
Welsh Office 17
Wansbeck 45
Wildlife Trusts 27
Wirral 25, 42
Woollen industry 2
World War, First and Second 3, 48, 61

York 2, 3
Yorkshire 2, 12, 23, 45

Printed in the UK for HMSO.
Dd.300910, 5/95, C30, 56-6734, 5673.